Navigating Change

Managing Project Risk

Harold Ainsworth

Published by KDi Asia Pte Ltd

www.kdiasia.com
www.kdi-americas.com

ISBN:
978-981-09-8598-1

Table of Contents

Table of Figures

PREFACE

Audience

This thin book is aimed at senior and middle managers who need to understand more about risk management for project investments. It may also serve as an introduction to new practitioners wishing to gain an overview of the topic. It is not a technical book suitable for practitioners of risk management who will need to seek further information about the processes and techniques involved.

It is my hope that this book will provide managers with greater understanding and more effective approaches to improving risk management in their organizations so that investment in projects are routinely successful.

Acknowledgements

Appreciation to those who have helped review material for this thin book including my colleagues Andrew Gunn, Terry Quanborough, Tan Kim Leng and Dr. Nancy Harkrider.

CHAPTER 1

Introduction

"All courses of action are risky, so prudence is not in avoiding danger (it's impossible), but calculating risk and acting decisively. Make mistakes of ambition and not mistakes of sloth. Develop the strength to do bold things, not the strength to suffer." (Niccolo Machiavelli, The Prince (1513))

Background

In his excellent book, "Against the Gods – The remarkable story of Risk" (1996, 2008), Peter Bernstein traces the history of risk management from the earliest times to the modern day, starting with people consulting the Oracle at the temple by killing a goat and examining the entrails to chart the appropriate course of action - to the modern more quantitative approach using probability analysis. He explains how probability theory was developed over a long period of time, a fascinating study in its own right, and applied to various situations we encounter involving risk, including modern day insurance.

Today our understanding of risk has become much more sophisticated, and often quantified, although we do need to be careful we don't become awed by the numbers. I remember some years ago being on an international flight and having time to watch a documentary about the Global Financial Crisis (GFC) that started in the 2007-2008 timeframe. They were interviewing a senior banker who admitted they really believed that through their sophisticated

1

quantitative modeling they had actually completely removed the risks in the financial instruments they were selling.

I found this startling since if they had explained their position to a first year university student in layman's language as to exactly what they were doing, I have no doubt that intuitively the student would have quickly identified tremendous risk. The bankers had become blind to it through their sophisticated modeling and we suffered the consequences.

While intuition can be helpful at times it can also lead us astray. As Tali Sharot, a neuroscientist tells us in her book "The Optimism Bias" (2011), we are hardwired to be optimists, as shown in brain scans. More later on this topic. While this optimism can be useful for the development of the human race by causing us to undertake risky but innovative ventures, it can also lead us astray and this is why effective risk management can assist us to be more anchored and discerning.

What Risk Management Addresses

Today we live in an increasingly complex environment, no longer local but very much global, so that what happens in one part of the world can often affect us quickly. We also live in a world where technology is changing at a rapid pace. So there is a lot of uncertainty when we decide to invest in new initiatives which typically we call "projects" or sometimes "programs".

Risk management helps us to deal with some of this uncertainty and one of the terms we use for these risks is "known unknowns". By that we mean that we can identify potential events that will impact on the outcomes of our projects, and we can determine some likelihood of this event occurring, and also assess what we believe its impact will be.

There is another level of uncertainty of events which we call "unknown unknowns" and risk management will not help us here since we do not even know what the event might be, and therefore have no way of assessing a likelihood or level of impact. We will mention more on this later.

Uncertainty can have both upsides and downsides, or as some people call it "positive risks" or opportunities, so there is a tendency these days to also look for the opportunities created by uncertainty, and to try and optimize them wherever we are able.

Most of this book will deal with traditional risk management, although you will discover there are some special types of messy and wicked risks that will need a different type of approach.

Project Success

Years ago projects tended to be judged successful if we delivered mostly on time and approximately on budget and created the original scope. However, in recent times we have realized this is not sufficient and that what we really need to achieve is the original planned outcomes from our investment.

A good example of this, although certainly a mega project by any standard, is the Channel Tunnel between England and France. A very complex undertaking and there is a lot of material available on the Internet on this project, and many issues to be considered when deciding whether this was a success or not. Without getting into a lot of detail, may I suggest that from a technology point of view it was a marvelous piece of engineering of unparalleled proportions when you consider the obstacles that they were facing. However, from an economic or financial perspective it was not a success. It will take very many decades at least for the investors to recoup their money.

There are major reasons for this. Firstly there were significant cost overruns, secondly they did not count on the competition from budget airlines and the ferries dropping their prices, and thirdly it was another decade before the British Government developed the promised high-speed rail link between London and the Tunnel to make it attractive for travelers to use the Tunnel. Now the criteria for success has broadened and this is another reason risk management today needs to cover not just technical or delivery risk but the broader economic, environmental and social issues.

How Organizations Approach Risk

Where I live in Australia there has been increasing interest in risk management in recent years. Some large organizations have appointed Chief Risk Officers, or established a corporate risk management office, and are undertaking what today is called Enterprise Risk Management (ERM) which looks across all major activities in the organization including their operations to understand the risks and to manage them better. One of the professional organizations that I belong to is the Governance Institute of Australia and they have a significant focus on risk, conducting training sessions for managers, discussion forums and regular articles in their professional journal.

However, even smaller organizations need to consider risk management at all levels, both operational and investments in new undertakings. You may have a successful business today, and it can very quickly be lost or crippled when a competitor starts up their business using a different business model, often based on the internet.

If you are submitting a business case, project justification or proposal to undertake a new project initiative, most organizations will require an initial risk analysis at that stage. However, there is a feeling that in some organizations risk management is more of a "tick the box" exercise, and once the analysis is performed for the project justification you can "get on with the real work" of execution and delivery. This is unfortunate and I have seen situations like this which have meant project failure because events occurred and by the time the project responded to them it was too late.

In other organizations risk management is part of the culture and risks are reviewed before new ventures are launched, in order that appropriate management plans can be put in place. One of the project services organizations I worked for years ago took risk management very seriously, with the result that they were able to undertake leading-edge technology development and be successful. As long as we understood the risks, and allowed for them and managed them at an appropriate cost, it did not prevent us from moving ahead with the project. So risk management can be quite powerful in enabling the organization to be innovative and successful.

Some organizations will tell you they do not give much attention to risk management, as it is a negative and they would prefer to focus on the positives. There is often a very strong culture there to be positive. While there are a lot of benefits in taking a positive stance, it is still best to do this once you have understood what the potential downsides might be. While risk management may be seen as negative, it is also quite powerful in enabling you to tackle exciting new ventures that you would otherwise not consider and be successful. There is nothing more disempowering than to work in an organization where there are constant project failures and people are pushed to breaking point due to the lack of adequate planning for potential negative incidents.

There are many examples of poor risk management and in the Appendix are a number of links to websites listed where you can obtain case studies about project failures, many of them due to poor risk management.

We will talk later about ways to embed risk management as part of the culture of the organization, which I acknowledge is not easy to do, but very beneficial. This is not just about having a lot of processes in the organization to manage risk, as some organizations have these processes but are still very risk-averse or incompetent in managing risk. These processes need to be supported by trained and competent staff and the appropriate culture based on openness and trust.

Today in organizations that deal with hazardous material or activities which involve personal safety there is a strong focus on this aspect of risk management, both for reasons of compliance with regulations, and also because the company wants to be a good citizen and have a safe workplace for their employees.

There are numerous books and articles written on risk management, and quite a number of organizations selling software tools to help you manage risk.

Case Studies

As we progress we will reference some case studies to help make the concepts more concrete. A number of them will be government sector related, simply because it is easier to obtain information about such failures. Typically an Auditor-General will investigate and publish a report which is placed on the Internet and available to all readers. However, private organizations do have their fair share of risky projects that fail fully or partially but the information is less likely to come into the public domain.

Almost two decades ago a significant technical University in Australia decided to implement a new Student Administration System based on a package from an overseas supplier. It was a new approach including web-based enrollments due to go live in October 2001. However, the risks were not handled and the cost increased to $47million which was 3 times the original budget. There were delays in enrolling students, with a subsequent drop in future student numbers and corrupted University records . Finally the system had to be scrapped and replaced and the government Education Minister ordered an audit report, with the result that the University President resigned. So apart from the damage to the University's budgets and student enrolments, there was significant collateral reputational damage. The Auditor's report listed a number of project management issues which good risk management should have identified, including lack of a fallback plan as problems emerged and identifying overall poor corporate level governance.

The Structure of this Thin Book is as Follows:

- Chapter 2 will provide some basic principles that we need to understand before undertaking risk management.
- Chapter 3 will take us through the steps of risk management and the various documents that will be produced.
- Chapter 4 will deal with some more advanced thinking around risk management including our bias for optimism which can get in the way.
- Chapter 5 will deal with how we can improve the way our organizations manage risk, and even if we are doing it reasonably well there is always room for further improvement.
- Chapter 6 will be some concluding thoughts and pointers for future development.

Endnotes

- Bernstein, Peter (1996 & 2008) *Against the Gods – The remarkable story of Risk*, John Wiley & sons, New York
- Sharot, Tali (2011) *The Optimism Bias - A Tour of the Irrationally Positive Brain,* Pantheon Books, New York

CHAPTER 2

Basic Principles of Risk Management

"Everything that can be counted does not necessarily count; everything that counts cannot necessarily be counted." Albert Einstein

Risk Allocation

Today it has become quite common for project owners to transfer as much of the risk as possible to external parties such as suppliers and contractors. Many suppliers and contractors unfortunately have begun to accept these additional risks as they are desperate to win business. In such a situation the project owners have considerable negotiating power to push their agenda. However, once the contract is signed a lot of this power is lost and they can become beholden to the other party if they want the project completed.

There is an old but wise principle about risk allocation.

Risk should be carried by the party who is best able to control the risk AND who has the capacity to absorb the risk impact if the risk occurs.

The sensible approach is to discuss the risks and who is the most appropriate party to bear these risks, and if it is the external party, understand that they will need to add a premium to their price to cover that risk. This occurs in some instances but unfortunately far too few, and project owners have become very used to "bullying" external parties to accept unreasonable risk. In many cases later it comes back on them in various ways, particularly if the external party does not have the capacity to absorb that risk.

I saw an instance of this years ago working for a project services provider where we bid $22 million to a state government agency in Australia to undertake a complex system development. The bid was won by our competitors for $17 million, but they had underestimated the difficulty of developing the system. Some years later they approached our company to see if we wanted to acquire them as they were on the verge of bankruptcy and their CEO told me this story during due diligence discussions. They had exhausted their project budget and not been able to complete the project, and advised the state government agency, who ended up granting them another $5 million as "variations" (they were not variations but miscalculation of effort by the contractor) to allow them to finish the job. The state government agency felt this was the better solution as they would end up with a finished product, whereas if the company went bankrupt the product may never be complete. This is not the only project that was suffering problems so we declined their offer of purchase since we would simply be inheriting a number of problems. In this case situation the risk that had been transferred to the external party had come back to impact the government agency when the external party did not have the capacity to absorb the risk of their own underestimation of the project cost. Government agencies are often compelled to comply with a "value for money" contract assessment model which should specifically include the implicit or explicit cost of risk management in the evaluation methodology.

Today enlightened project owners are looking for alternative approaches to risk sharing with external parties. It is not easy to do this well and will require the organizations involved to build up a level of trust and an effective working relationship, and I have seen it work well in the right circumstances. The table below gives an overview of some of the approaches that are used today to share risk with other parties.

Approach used	How risk is shared	Comments
Partnering	There are a number of approaches that can be used under these heading: • open book on costs, with or without a risk sharing pool. • shared risk register. • firm price, but allowing the other party the opportunity to fix problems as they eventuate without incurring penalties or being subject to litigation.	Has been used mostly successfully in the construction industry to reduce the adversarial relationships that are typical in these types of projects.
Target and ceiling price	• The contractor works to an agreed target price, which is lower than the ceiling price. • There is a ceiling price beyond which they cannot go, which is effectively a fixed price. • If the contractor meets the target price, or comes in less than the ceiling price, there is an agreed sharing of the difference between the target and ceiling price.	There will be certain conditions the supplier needs to meet (such as quality) in order to gain access to the shared bonus funds.

Approach used	How risk is shared	Comments
PPP (Public and Private Partnerships)	• Can take various forms including the BOOM type below. Designed to relieve Governments of finding the funding for projects and also transfers risk to the private sector. • Long life of the contract creates problems for both parties. Complex contracts required.	Mixed results with it sometimes working and others not so well. There is a concern that risk can also be transferred back to Government in some instances.
BOOM contracts (Build, Own, Operate and Maintain)	• The supplier invests their own money to build the product or service capability, which they operate and maintain on behalf of the end client. They absorb construction and financing risk. • Their revenue comes from transactions over a given lifecycle period (sometimes called concession), which is designed to recoup their initial outlay and produce a profit margin. • Depending on the arrangement at the end of the concession period the product or service capability is	Favored by government agencies in order to reduce the initial outlays on infrastructure. Sometimes the ultimate owner has to agree to certain restrictions to protect the BOOM party's revenue stream.

Approach used	How risk is shared	Comments
	transferred to the end-user / owner.	
Progressive pricing	• The supplier provides an order of magnitude or budgetary estimate for the whole scope of work, and a fixed price for the scoping or requirements definition. • After the requirements are defined, they provide a new budgetary estimate and a fixed price for the design. • After the design is complete they provide a fixed price for the build or execution phase.	Requires a sound relationship between the parties with a high level of trust and transparency to utilize this approach.

Risk Appetite

A term that we often hear today is the "risk appetite" of the organization. It alludes to the fact that some organizations are more risk-averse than others, and this will be reflected in their approach to risk management. It may also vary for different activities in the one organization. For example in Australia organizations engaged in the mining industry are heavily regulated because of health and safety factors. This is reflected in their approach to risk management both for compliance reasons and also because they want to be seen as a company that offers a safe working environment. Safety incidents are reported and analyzed and where serious injury or death occurs they are subject to internal and public investigations. These organizations have strict rules around staff being allowed into the workplace if there is any trace of drugs including alcohol on them, and this rule even applies in their offices which are far away from the mine sites. Bulletin boards in their offices record their record of safety and incidents. There is little tolerance to mistakes here but they may take larger risks in other areas not related to safety.

Organizations may set rules around what risks they are willing to take and under what circumstances. Working for a project services provider in the past our policy on commercial risks related to projects were:

- Liquidated damages for late delivery had to be capped at a percentage of the project, typically less than 10%;
- No unlimited liability or consequential damages accepted;
- No "time is of the essence clauses", as they gave the client too much power over us;
- Performance bonds were possible in certain circumstances but at a premium in our price.

So establishing risk thresholds for various activities helps project teams to perform effective risk management, for both suppliers and customers.

Balance Between Risk and Reward

Ultimately it all comes down to a balance between risk and reward. We do not want to be taking too much risk if the potential reward is inadequate. However, we do need to be aware that there is a strong tendency to:

- understate the costs of the initiative;
- and to overstate the benefits.

If the risks are not adequately factored into the cost / benefit equation it will distort our perception of risk and reward. If we are already emotionally committed to undertaking an initiative it is not difficult to "tweak" the numbers to provide justification for proceeding. There are many examples of public sector projects which are being undertaken on this basis, when the numbers did not support them. Bent Flyvbjerg (2002) has written on the issue of risk in large mega projects and says that there is ample evidence that the above understatement / overstatement scenario exists in public sector projects. I also believe it exists in private sector projects but less visible. This is why it is a sound principle to follow - that all cost and benefit estimates should be independently verified. This can be achieved by involving government agencies representatives from the agency's audit branch or the independent procurement branch in the evaluation of tenders. The same applies on large projects at certain key milestones when forecasting estimated time and cost to complete. There should be procedures to be followed for forecasting based on sound principles, and occasionally independently verified that these are being followed.

Ownership

If we want to ensure that actions are taken and the risks are monitored then we should be allocating it to a responsible person to own that risk. Sometimes there is a tendency to allocate a risk to a number of people which simply diffuses accountability and the desire to ensure action is taken. Also it is not a useful idea to have most of the risks allocated to the project manager, sponsor or a single person, but rather to spread them around various responsible people who have the knowledge and ability to make a difference. Risk owners need to be engaged and aware of their responsibilities.

Risk qualification versus quantification

My personal preference is to see risk quantified, since I believe it is easier for management to understand the risk profile of a project expressed in monetary terms. If the project manager says to the senior management this is a $1 million project but we require a contingency reserve because of the risks of $250k, it strikes me as more meaningful. Many organizations simply assess risk using a rating scale either 1-5 or very low, low, medium, high and very high. Also sometimes they then plot the risk in a risk matrix chart.

A Risk Matrix using this approach would look like the following although some version put numbers in each of the cells to give a more "quantitative rating"; (note this matrix is only 4x4 as the "very low" category has been eliminated as not worthy of consideration).

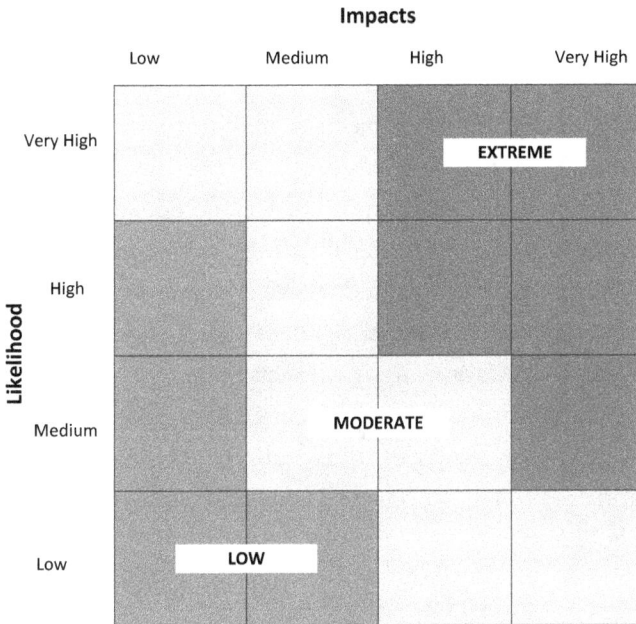

Figure 1 - Risk Matrix

Douglas Hubbard (2009) in his book sees these rating scales as "worse than useless" and misleading, which are very strong terms. Some of the key reasons he mentions are:

- These rating descriptions are understood differently by different people, even if attempts are made to standardize them;
- They introduce their own sources of error due to their structure;
- They are isolated from research and do not consider issues such as the intervals between the scales and presume a level of independence between the risks.

However, I believe they are still useful in the Risk Qualification step to identify those risks that deserve further treatment.

In certain types of public projects it may not always be possible to quantify risk in monetary terms and they may need to be expressed more in terms of outcomes desired. I came across this many years ago while doing some training in a public hospital context, where some of the criteria they wanted to use covered issues such as "High external impact - affects patient / client care, image in market place" and "Impacts on adoption by Clinicians in hospitals", which are harder to quantify in money terms. Risk quantification is difficult but the more precisely we can think about the risk the better we understand it, even if we change our views over time as we learn more.

Signals of Potential Failure

A question that is often asked is whether there are signals that would indicate a project is failing. It can depend very much on the type of project being conducted, however here are some generic indicators that might assist:

- Regular status performance reports are late or not very informative;
- There is inconsistency in key performance indicators - like the schedule is slipping but the budget is not, or the risk profile is increasing significantly but there is no impact on estimated time to complete or final cost;
- Answers to questions raised in Governance forums are not being quickly addressed;

- Contingency reserves, both budget and / or schedule, are being used at a rate greater than the progress through the project and will not suffice for the rest of the project;
- Significant risks at the start of the project are still showing the same likelihood / probability and impact, which would indicate that response actions do not appear to be effective.
- KPIs (key performance indicators) are ignored or not acted upon by Governance group members (e.g. steering committee, control boards), often due to project governance failure as a result of inadequate understanding of their roles and responsibilities.

It is sometimes thought by managers that only large and risky undertakings need to adopt risk management. However, even in small consulting assignments I find it necessary to consider what the risk may be, although not necessarily through a lot of formal documentation. For example on a small consulting assignment of $30k to 50k considerations may include:

- What are the client's expectations about deliverables? I try to define this in terms of a report of x number of pages and PowerPoint pack of y number of slides, and sometimes with a potential table of contents to clarify coverage;
- If the client has a particular end date in mind, clarify that they need to make timely decisions and turnaround draft documents within z days of their submission for review;
- Clarify what access is required to certain people, documents websites etc.;
- Describe the intermediate milestones and deliverables.

All these issues can be documented in a proposal or exchange of emails to ensure both parties have a similar understanding of scope and methods to avoid disappointment and even dispute at the end of the assignment.

Reflections

- A fair allocation of risk based on sound principles will result in a better outcome for all parties, rather than trying to pass all of the risk to the party with the least negotiating power;
- There is a balance between risk and reward but in order to understand this both the costs and the benefits need to be reasonably accurate to allow objective assessment and not manipulated to produce a desired outcome;
- Understand the organization's "risk appetite" for the type of activity being undertaken to ensure alignment with the organization's goals in this area;
- Each risk should have a single owner, and spread the ownership amongst responsible parties not just the project manager or sponsor. Risk owners need to be clear on their responsibilities;
- For many activities quantifying risk will help to understand it better, although in some instances a qualified measure may be more appropriate. Be aware of the limitation of risk rating or scoring measures.

Endnotes

- Bruzelius, N Flyvbjerg, B Rothengatter, W (2002) "Bid decisions, big risks. Improving accountability in mega projects", *Transport Policy*, 9, 143-154

- Flyvbjerg, B, Holm, M S, & Buhl, S (2002), "Underestimating Cost in Public Works Projects- Error or Lie?, *Journal of the American Planning Association*, Vol. 68, No. 3, Summer, pp. 279-295
- Hubbard, Douglas (2009) *"The Failure of Risk Management – Why it is broken and how to fix it"*, John Wiley & sons, Hoboken, NJ

CHAPTER 3

Risk Management Steps and Outputs Produced

"People who don't take risks generally make about two big mistakes a year. People who do take risks generally make about two big mistakes a year." (Peter F. Drucker – Management guru and author)

The Steps to Risk Management
(Note that various standards might use slightly different terminology but they are all interchangeable)

The following table is a summary of a more detailed one in Resources at end of the book.

Activity	Possible approaches	Output	Who is involved
Plan Risk Management (define how to conduct risk management activities for the specific project)	Analytical techniques. Meetings.	Risk Management Plan. Decision on Risk Register Template to be used.	PM
Identify Risks (determine risks affecting the project & document characteristics)	Document Reviews. Checklists. Brainstorming. Facilitated Workshops. Historical data.	Unqualified list of all identified risks placed into Risk Register.	PM & Team Sponsor Stakeholders

Activity	Possible approaches	Output	Who is involved
Perform Qualitative Risk Analysis	Rating Assessment criteria. Checklists. Risk Matrix.	Updated Risk Register with qualified list of risks with probability & impact documented. Impact areas also documented e.g. cost, schedule, performance etc. Some risks identified for further treatment.	PM & Team
Perform Quantitative Risk Analysis	What if planning including: Critical Path Method, Delphi Technique Historical Data, EMV, Decision trees	Quantified List of Risk in Risk Register – i.e. Factored Risks using expected monetary value (EMV).	PM & Team
Plan Risk Responses	Normal Risk strategies. Checklist. Brain-storming. Historical Data. Peer review.	Updated Risk Plan / Risk Register with mitigations/actions etc. Budgets for mitigation and contingency – in Project Plan. Estimated residual risk after treatment. Contingency plans if risk occurs.	PM & Team Independent Reviewer
Control Risks	Frequent Review of Risk Register. Review effectiveness of mitigations.	Updated Risk Register Status Reports with Risk status.	PM Team Sponsor Stakeholders

Activity	Possible approaches	Output	Who is involved
Baseline Risk Plan and Register		Project Approval – Key Risk sheet. Approved Project Plan with Risk Register. Approved Risk Plan.	PM Sponsor Stakeholders

Some notes on the above

Risk Plan: A Risk Plan describes the approach to risk management to be used for the project, however if the organization already has appropriate processes the plan may simply reference these processes unless they are going to deviate from them. The Risk Plan may for smaller projects be a section of the overall Project Plan.

Sources of Risk: There are many potential sources and the Risk Breakdown structure will help to identify various categories. Assumptions are a major source of risk and should be documented and examined carefully. Possible sources of risk will include schedule, cost, deliveries by external parties, quality control, materials and equipment, legal and commercial which are usually covered in contracts, people resources, technology, project structure, financing, political events, natural events, high operational performance requirements etc.

Risk Breakdown Structure: They look like an organization chart which is decomposed and are used today to categorize risk under various headings (typically 5 or more major "buckets") and help us to ensure that we have covered all the potential risk categories. People will tend to focus on the risks that they understand best. Technical people will obviously focus on technical types of risks, and the project team on delivery risks, so it is important to have a wide range of stakeholders involved to obtain a comprehensive view of risks. Sometimes risk that the delivery team sees are not that important to management who will see different risks at a corporate level.

Risk Register: Rather than provide a template it is better to provide a list of potential content for a risk register, which may be in the form of an Excel spreadsheet unless you are using some database type tool.

Description	Comments
Risk Number	For identification purposes
Risk Identification Date	Date the risk was identified
Risk Description	Full risk description
Risk Category	Categories of risk and include technical, delivery, legal, supplier etc.
Risk Probability / Likelihood	Can be in the form of the probability percentage or some use ratings like low medium and high
Risk Impact	Impact of the risk - ideally quantified in monetary terms
Risk Response Action Plan	The plans to contain the risk and reduce the likelihood of it occurring
Risk Contingency Plan	The plan if the risk occurs to try and recover from it
Risk Owner	Person who is responsible for ensuring the risks plans are taken and for monitoring the status
Current Status	Open or closed
Date of Last Risk Review	Date when the risk was last reviewed

Description	Comments
Optional	
Risk Trigger	Some event or measure that would indicate the risk is very likely to occur shortly
EMV (Expected Monetary Value)	Calculated as probability times the impact value e.g. (70% * 1,000 = $700)
Residual Risks Probability	The probability of the risk occurring after response / containment actions have been conducted
Residual EMV	Residual risk probability times the impact value
Dependencies	Links to other risks that influence mitigation, treatment or priority of treatment

It is important to have **good descriptions of risk** which are not broad or vague. For example to describe the risk as being "the lack of good communications on the project will lead to problems later on" is meaningless. What do we mean by lack of good communications and what do we mean by problems? The risk description should include the possible event, some indication of timing, and clarity about the likely impact. It is only then that we can start to determine its likelihood or probability and calculate the seriousness of the impact and ideally the impact monetary value.

Some risk registers will ask for a **Risk trigger** to be provided, which is a clear measure which when it occurs indicates a high likelihood that the risk will occur very soon. By using risk triggers we are starting to define potential events more clearly and precisely.

Response Versus Contingency: One of the topics that causes some confusion to the novice is the difference between responding to the risk as a preventative control, for which we use the words containment and sometimes loosely the word mitigation, and contingency plans which are those actions taken if the risk should occur.

An example of a response would be to try and transfer the risk through contract terms to another party, or to increase the level of expertise on the project to reduce the likelihood of the risk occurring. Contingency plans which will be initiated if the risk happens could include moving to a fallback plan, or bringing on additional resources to help recover some of the lost schedule time.

Many years ago the project services organization I worked for had a high risk project which was utilizing some software technology which was still very new and we were using it to develop a new banking system for a client. The project manager had a fallback plan that at a certain point in time if we were falling behind utilizing the new technology, he planned to revert to a more traditional technology in order to avoid major delays. Fortunately we did not have to revert to the fallback plan and were able to deliver successfully to the client very close to our original budget and schedule. Things that worked in our favor were that we had a competent and high performing team, and we had undertaken significant upfront planning to ensure that we knew how we were going to approach the use of the new technology, including adequate training.

Risk Quantification: The process above assumes that risk will be quantified at least to an EMV (expected monetary value) which may then be used to calculate a budget contingency, but it is recognized that not everybody will do this. However, when determining impact some will use schedule or cost impact criteria to determine the ratings. For example:

Rating	Schedule impact	Budget impact
Very high	Greater than 4 week schedule slip	$100,000
High	3 to 4 week schedule slip	$50,000–$100,000
Medium	2 to 3 week schedule slip	$25,000–$50,000
Low	1 to 2 week schedule slip	$10,000–$25,000
Very Low	Less than 1 week schedule slip	less than $10,000

The values in above table need to be tailored to the typical projects undertaken by the organization.

The above approach I believe has limitations since the ranges can be quite large and a more correct and appropriate method is to calculate the impact through analyzing the cost of the changes required to attempt to address the problem.

For example, if we take a relatively simple problem such as Event X causes a schedule delay of 2 months and to attempt to recover some of this time we add resources.

- Resource A for 10 days @ $500 per day
- Resource B for 15 days @ $500 per day
- Resource C for 5 days @ $700 per day
- TOTAL cost impact is $16k

Having produced a Risk Register with probability, impacts and EMV's it is not simply a matter of adding up the total of the EMV to determine the contingency, as shown in the simple example below.

Risk	Probability	Impact $ k	EMV $ k
A	.5	500	250
B	.6	300	180
C	.7	150	105

Total EMV of these risks is $535 k but in a risk register consisting of maybe 20 or more risks there will be further analysis required such as:

- Can any of the risks be transferred to other parties and to what extent?
- Are there any risks which have the same impact and therefore we would not want to double up by allowing for multiple occurrences of the same impact;
- We also need to consider what is the highest risk impact before we apply the probability, since if this risk occurs it is the impact amount not the EMV that will be required to rectify the problem;
- Are there any risk scenarios or chained or linked risks, which is a situation where one risk occurs and has a knock on or domino effect on a number of other risks. In this case we need to consider the total cumulative impact of the total chain or scenario;
- We can also apply the effects of risk responses and determine contingency based on residual risk as discussed later in this chapter.

So further analysis and judgment is required to determine budget contingency.

There are also other techniques such as Regression Analysis, Method of the Moments, and Monte Carlo simulation of the budget, but all of these plus the above approach will have limitations in various ways. So it is best not to seek for a perfect solution but to find one that suits your organizational situation and the availability of appropriate information. Setting contingency is not an exact science and requires judgement on the part of management, but is certainly and improvement on the commonly bused "let us just add 10% for good measure" approach.

Outputs of the Process: The key outputs from the process above is a risk register containing the risks that we are going to manage throughout the project. The risk register will identify the preventative action plans and ideally the contingency plans if the risk occurs. The register will also be important to the calculations whereby we derive a budget and a schedule contingency. There should be both budget and schedule contingency, which does not always occur, since if you have the budget you also need allowance in the schedule to be able to utilize it.

The control of these contingency reserves is often intensely debated, with some organizations removing them from the project manager's control. My personal view is that the project manager should have control over them, however should advise on their usage each reporting period. Others believe that if you allow this level of control contingency will always be used up, but that may also depend on how you assess the project managers performance. If it is not under project manager's control then they should have quick access to the senior manager who does control it.

Contingency reserves need to be carefully managed and as a general "rule of thumb" you would expect them to be used at a lesser rate than the progress through the project. In other words if the project is 50% complete you expect that normally contingency would be less than 50% utilized. As the project proceeds there is often a tendency particularly with budget contingency for finance people to want to reclaim unused contingency for other purposes. It will be up to the project manager to justify why they still need the current level of contingency available based on a conservative view.

I was involved as an external consultant to a major program some years ago where the Program Director allowed the finance people to remove most of his remaining contingency, despite my clear warning about one of their key suppliers. As I predicted the key supplier could not deliver on time and there was a three-month slippage. The program team had to sit around doing little until the supplier finally delivered. Contingency funds would have covered this event but was no longer available.

<u>Schedule Contingency:</u> Sometimes projects have budget contingency but no schedule contingency, but in order to be able to utilize budget contingency you also need some schedule contingency. There is less clarity around methods for schedule contingency however I do believe that David Hulett's approach (Hulett, 2011) in his most recent book is well considered. In essence you take a resource loaded schedule, and also add in the costs, and major risks are allocated to key activities (in some cases you may need a summarized schedule rather than a detailed schedule). Some risks can impact on more than one activity and some activities will have several risks impacting on them. He then uses Monte Carlo simulation, for which you do need a specialized software tool, to analyze the results. However, I have my students use the PERT formula (Program Evaluation & Review Technique) and Excel spreadsheet to simulate this for a case study project, and although it is not as accurate, it at least demonstrates the principles involved. The advantage of Hulett's approach is the both cost and schedule are considered together and as he demonstrates in his book the resulting budget contingency is often higher when an

integrated approach is taken, since schedule risk can impact on cost and vice versa, something which many organizations fail to consider. There are some papers available on the internet that explain the essence of his approach but his book is a worthwhile read for the project practitioner.

Monitoring and Reporting on Risk: This should be occurring at regular intervals, usually for each reporting period. It will include assessing whether the risk response actions are being taken and their effectiveness, and also the likelihood and the impact of the risk should be regularly re-assessed. Also there should be a scanning to see if there are any new risks arising which were not previously identified. It is useful to also go back to the initial list of risks identified, some of which were discarded as being either low likelihood or low impact and not worth while being managed. Have any of these risks changed such that they should now be included?

Calculate the amount of contingency required to cover current risk to the end of the project. Advise on its adequacy or otherwise in the status report.

While projects will take actions to respond to potential risk to try and prevent, contain or mitigate either the likelihood or the impact, we know that sometimes these actions are not as effective as hoped they might be. Therefore for significant risks it is suggested that there should be more than one prevention or containment actions taken, in case the single action is not effective. Also this is sometimes called "escalation" where prevention actions are not as effective as first believed, in which case another preventative action is initiated, but it will require constant monitoring of the containment actions to assess their effectiveness and the need for further action.

I once had to review a failed project to ascertain where it had gone wrong. My first question to the project manager was "did you have a risk register" to which he answered "yes". My next question was "did you regularly review it" to which his answer was "no, it was put in the drawer and forgotten". Resourcing of the team with appropriate expertise by the supplier was a key issue and not monitored. When the external supplier failed to deliver a working product, the project manager probably in ignorance, did not document this sufficiently, and the procurement department that was meant to provide oversight also did not become involved. By the time the legal team became involved it was decided that the chances of successful litigation were minimal and the client/owner was forced to write the investment off as a loss.

Project team meetings should regularly include time to review risks and discuss any changes in circumstances perhaps as frequently as on a daily or weekly basis, depending on how volatile the circumstances may be.

Residual Risk is the risk remaining after the treatment or response actions have been taken, and some organizations like to calculate this in order to determine the level of contingency. This is perfectly acceptable but my concern is that you establish an initial probability, which is difficult enough, and then need to establish another probability as a result of the treatment actions. Sometimes this can be a little precarious. I suspect it depends on the level of confidence you have in the initial probability and the calculation of the residual probability.

To illustrate the above point here is a very simple example of Residual Risk calculations:

Risk	Probability	Impact $ k	EMV $ k	New Probability after response	New Impact after response	Residual EMV
A	.5	500	250	.25	250	62.5
B	.6	300	180	.3	180	54
C	.7	150	105	.6	100	60

In the above example we would use the Residual EMV instead of the original EMV to calculate budget contingency as outlined in Risk Quantification section above.

How Many Risks? As you will note from the table above the first step is to identify a large number and wide range of risks, which are then qualified in order to determine those to be managed. The result should be a smaller number of risks that will be subject to quantification and regular management. The Oresund Bridge between Denmark and Sweden, a very significant infrastructure project, at the time it was built (around 2000) was a 2.5 billion USD project and they decided to manage between 50-100 risks based on those that had the greatest cost impact on the project. I am sure that a project of this magnitude could have identified many more risks to be managed. However, by focusing on the most critical ones they had a relatively successful project, at least in delivery terms, although the revenue from traffic were not so positive in the early stages.

In reducing the risks to a manageable number we should still be careful to recognize **low probability but high impact type risks**. We should at least keep a watching brief on them, even though the probability may initially be low, since if they do occur their impact on the project can be quite significant.

Reflections

In this chapter we have considered:

- The key steps in risk management in order to give the manager an overview of the activities that will be undertaken by the project manager and the team, in conjunction with key stakeholders;
- It is absolutely essential that stakeholders are involved as they will have a different but important perspective on risk compared to the project team. They also need to be involved throughout the life of the project at regular intervals to review progress of risk management;
- Risk management continues throughout the life of the project, both in monitoring existing risks and plans for their treatment, and watching for new risks or changes in risks that may occur;
- The relevance of budget and schedule contingency to allow for the unexpected, and the need to carefully manage and conserve it.
- Have a manageable number of risks that are important to the project's success;
- Risk management is a day to day activity for project managers and should be a natural part of discussions at regular team meetings.

Endnotes

- See the relevant standards listed in the Resources
- Hulett, D (2011) *"Integrated Cost – Schedule Risk Analysis"*, Gower, Farnham, UK

- Oresund Bridge – there are articles on the internet, Wikipedia and also a number of videos on You Tube covering this project. One overview article is
  https://en.wikipedia.org/wiki/%C3%98resund_Bridge

CHAPTER 4

Other Thoughts on Risk

"The first principle is that you must not fool yourself, and you are the easiest person to fool." (Richard P. Feynman, Nobel Prize–winning physicist and author)

Not All risks are the Same

What we have been discussing in the previous chapters relates to the standard approach to risk management, which has grown out of traditional project management both in construction and in more recent years around business and information technology type projects. However, there is a growing recognition that many of our projects and initiatives today have become complicated and even complex. I do draw a distinction between these terms although many people will use them interchangeably.

An example of these different types of projects can be found on page 40 following:

	Mintzberg*	Business IT systems	Infrastructure
Simple	Build a pleasure boat	Build a simple database of customer information	Build a house
Complicated	Build an aircraft carrier	Link this database to multiple other legacy systems	Fit-out a multi-story office block
Complex	Deploy a warship	Deploy a Customer Relationship Management system (CRM)	Build a mega - shopping mall in Dubai

* (Mintzberg, 2004)

Complicated requires a lot of detailed planning by experts in each of the knowledge domains. There will be quite a bit of work in ensuring adequate interfaces between the expert's areas.

Complex is where we are not quite certain when we combine components together of what the final outcome might be, since the whole is not necessarily the sum of the parts. There are so many interrelationships that it is impossible to predict everything.

David Hancock (2010) in his book *Tame, Messy and Wicked Risk Leadership* describes these complex projects as having messy and wicked risks. Traditional risk management deals with simple and complicated situations, but is not necessarily appropriate when dealing with complex problems. His diagram below illustrates the types of risk and their treatment.

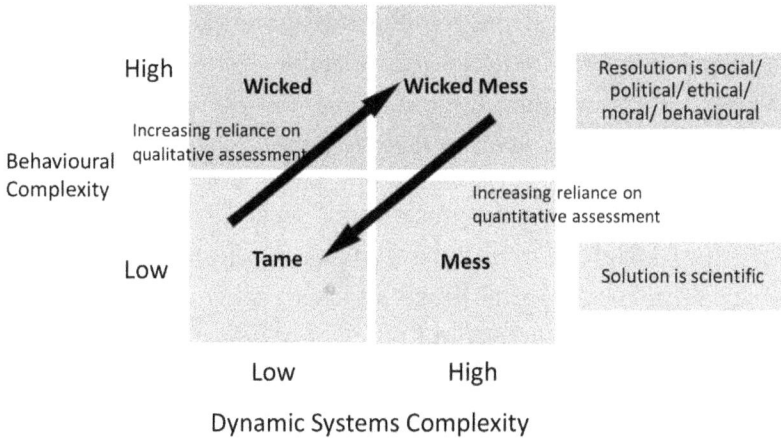

Figure 2 - Relationship Between Four Problem Types and Risk

Messy risks have high levels of systems complexity and wicked risks have high levels of behavioral complexity. Systems complexity = Complex levels of system interaction, especially when we consider the broader system in which the problem resides.

Behavioral complexity = Diversity of opinions, mental models and values of the key decision makers and characterized by deep disagreement in assumptions and beliefs.

His book provides the example of the building of Terminal 5 at Heathrow Airport and says that "Terminal 5 underwent an entire identity shift, from a technically constructed asset owned by a single company to a transport interchange invested in by many stakeholders" (Hancock & Holt, 2003). In other words it had gone from being complicated to quite complex, and with a number of key stakeholders with different agendas and desired outcomes. As such, the focus of risk management needed to change to more collaboration, which is harder to achieve and takes more time. Collaboration is a word that is regularly used in many situations, but

41

often very loosely and the resulting collaboration is far from ideal. Real collaboration requires considerable effort so that every stakeholder has a similar understanding and can agree on both the outcomes and how to achieve them together.

As we can see from the diagram above "wicked" and "wicked mess" type risks which have more behavioral complexity need to be handled by social, political, ethical moral and behavioral approaches rather than the more quantitative and procedural driven risk management that we would traditionally apply.

Opportunity Management

Uncertainty in projects and also programs can come in a number of forms such as uncertainty of objectives, priorities, estimates, approach/process, logistics, design, relationships between parties, etc. While these create risks they also create opportunities to do things differently or better.

For example:

- Substituting one "technology" for another, which could produce the same results but either better quality, less expensive or less maintenance;
- Cost or schedule reduction, change the scope (increase or reduce or use different approach) to include some new aspects/features/functions etc. that will bring benefits over the original plan;
- Also market/customer opportunity.

PMBoK (PMI, 2012) suggests these possible responses to opportunities.

Response	Description	Examples
Exploit	To ensure the opportunity is realized	Assign organization's most talented resources to the project or utilize new technology
Enhance	Increase the probability and/or positive impacts of an opportunity	Adding resources to finish early
Share	Allocating some or all of the ownership to a third party	Joint ventures, risk sharing partnerships
Accept	Willing to take advantage if it comes along, but not actively pursuing it	No specific examples

So, while keeping a strong focus on how risk can impact on the project, also keep an eye out for opportunities created by uncertainty that can be turned into positives.

"The Optimism Bias"

This is the name of the book by a neuroscientist, Tali Sharot (2011), and on YouTube there are a number of videos of her explaining the concept. Also here is a quote from her book.

"While the past few years have seen important advances in the neuroscience of optimism, one enduring puzzle remained. How is it that people maintain this rosy bias even when information challenging our upbeat forecasts is so readily available? Only recently have we been able to decipher this mystery, by scanning the brains of people as they process both positive and negative information about the future. The findings are striking: when people learn, their neurons faithfully encode desirable information that can enhance optimism but fail at incorporating unexpectedly

undesirable information."

(Source: http://www.guardian.co.uk/science/2012/jan/01/tali-sharot-the-optimism-bias-extract)

I am sure that optimism has been very instrumental in helping the human race to progress with various people taking risks in order to innovate and develop new ideas. Some people are very comfortable in that role, but if you are dealing with other people's money (and time) then some caution is required. Risk management helps us to do this especially by testing assumptions that underlie our estimates and our plans. All plans are built on the assumption that certain things will or will not happen, but we would be wise to check these in detail before launching out. In any group they will be certain people who have optimistic traits so instead of just following the lead we should be trying to understand how they arrived at the estimates and plans for the venture. By understanding these and planning potential actions at least then when events do not go according to plan we can respond more quickly and hopefully retrieve the situation.

There are a number of ways that we can do this:

- Edward de Bono came up with the idea of the 6 Thinking Hats (De Bono, 1985 & 1999) and the idea is that at least one person in the group should be assigned to play a "devil's advocate" type role and argue against the proposal;
- Of a similar nature is the idea of having someone put up an alternative proposal to help us understand better what our options might be, including the option of doing nothing at all;
- Another approach is that all assumptions should be documented and that we should search these for ones that have a significant impact if they do not occur. These will form

the basis of our initial risk analysis and be subject to further investigation.

The key issue here is that we should all be aware that we are subject to bias, not just optimism but other common biases including:

- The way in which the problem is framed;
- The availability (including frequency) of information;
- Tendency to be selective and listen to information that supports our pre-existing views (confirmation bias);
- Failure to consider the base rate or distribution within the population being examined (so we revert to stereotypes);
- Anchoring toward an initial position;
- Psychological tendency to minimize losses rather than maximize gains;
- Extrapolation from small or unrepresentative samples.

At least if we are very conscious of the above we can take steps to be more careful in how we process information.

Escalation and Sunk Costs

Related to the idea of optimism is the problem that when projects begin to appear to be failing, rather than consider withdrawing from the initiative and cease spending money, there a tendency to "escalate" our commitment to the project and spend even more time and money. Mark Keil (2000), has written extensively on this topic in various places and analyzed why it occurs. Part of the reason for this is the emotion involved of releasing ourselves from the effort and money already spent on the project. The "optimism bias" kicks in and we believe that we have found the answer to the problem and that from here-after everything will proceed smoothly and according to plan. Unfortunately, experience shows that this is very rarely the case and that more money and time is spent before we are forced to acknowledge failure. This is also known as the "sunk cost syndrome" which relates to our inability to write off the existing investment, so therefore we just keep investing more money in the futile hope that it will somehow come good in the future.

I was told by someone who works in the oil and gas industry that their company had spent $25 million building a processing plant as a prototype and proof of concept. They came to the conclusion it would not work so they scrapped it. It looks like $25 million wasted! However, their budget for the plant if they had proceeded, was $1.25 billion, so it was better to spend and discard $25 million rather than to discover later that the new plant would not be successful.

Risk Scenarios

The point I wish to make here is that risks are not all independent of each other and we need to understand how a number of them can combine in a scenario. Usually it is due to a cascading effect where one risk has a knock on effect to other risks. We have probably all seen this in one form or another. Sometimes it is also difficult to fully understand in advance what these connections might be, although in hindsight when we analyze the situation it is easier to understand. Charles Perrow, (Perrow, 1999) in his book Normal Accidents, talks about highly coupled systems especially in high technology industries such as nuclear power plants, oil and gas installations where if one event occurs it can quickly cause further events before operators can respond. I believe the BP Deepwater Horizon Oil Rig accident in the Gulf of Mexico was one of these situations, but I have also seen it occur in other circumstances on a less significant scale, but nonetheless damaging to the specific project objectives either of time, cost or outcomes.

Similarly with low probability but high impact risks, we need to be careful since if they do occur the impact can be very significant even though the initial probability was low and we did not give it is much attention in the first instance.

So for management it is not just about knowing that there is a comprehensive risk register and a recommended contingency of schedule and budget to cover potential risk events, but also understanding what could happen if a number of these related risks occurred due to a knock on or domino effect. Risk scenarios raise the overall level of risk so need to be carefully considered at a management level who will have a more comprehensive picture of the project and its inter-dependencies with other initiatives. Often it is judgment that identifies these scenarios based either on experience or thinking carefully about the interdependencies.

Dealing with Unknown Unknowns (called "unks unks")

"Unknown unknowns" (see quote by Rumsfeld, 2002) could be defined as "we do not know what we do not know" and therefore cannot be treated with traditional risk management approaches. Loch, Solt and Bailey (2008) and others have written books and articles on the topic and the table below shows their ideas to dealing with these types of uncertainty.

Management approaches to responding to Unknown Unknowns		Complexity	
		Low	High
Unforeseeable Uncertainty (Gaps in knowledge)	High	Trial-and-error learning: *Flexibility to fundamentally redefine the business plan and venture model*	Selectionism: after full information: *Best trial selected only after unknowns become known; e.g. after full-blown market tests*
	Low	Planning: *Execute target business plan with risk management: i.e. using buffers and modifications or contingency plan*	Selectionism: *Parallel trials with ex-post selection of best outcome*

(Loch et al, 2008)

In the lower left-hand cell is the traditional risk management approach; while in the upper left-hand cell is trial and error approach and the potential to redefine what we are planning to do based on our learning as we progress.

In the lower right-hand cell is what they call "selectionism" or running several trials in parallel to determine a suitable approach, and in the upper right-hand cell is waiting for more information to become available before making a final decision. This is similar to other approaches of dealing with complexity such as David Snowden's (see endnotes) "probe –sense-respond" approach to discovering what works and what does not in different problem spaces. He categorizes problems into four key areas of "known", "knowable" (or complicated), "complex" and "chaotic" in order to apply the relevant response, since applying in-appropriate responses is not productive. These approaches requires time and funds to experiment, both of which are often in short supply.

Now while all of this sounds like common sense, the reality is that often organizations do not stop and consider deeply the environment in which they are operating, which if they did they would possibly consider alternative approaches such as the ones described below. It means for example looking very closely at alternatives and this is meant to happen in proposals and business cases by considering various options including the "do nothing" option. It is often given minimal attention and has sometimes been described to me as a "tick the box" exercise as the solution being proposed has effectively been committed to by various parties who are simply going through the "show case" of looking at other alternatives.

As I noted earlier that one of the project services companies I worked for previously was very competent and could undertake very complex technology projects. Our systems for estimating and project management worked very well most of the time. However on one occasion we were caught out. We were asked by the client to quote on developing a new system for them. Our firm quote was around $250k (1980 prices) and we proceeded to assemble the team and do the work. It was a top team with a very competent project manager. We quickly found it was more difficult than expected and our final cost was $500k, since we had underestimated the business complexity of the requirements as it had never been built before anywhere in the world. The client was very happy with what we delivered and identified some changes to improve the system, which we undertook at a premium and were able to recover a small part of our losses. The lesson for us was if you have never built anything like that before then you need to be very careful as you probably do not really understand it.

As Fred Brooks (1975), who was the Project Manager of some of the early computer operating systems noted, the best way to build a system, is build one and throw it away, and then develop the proper one because now you understand what you are creating. In those days operating systems were very much the leading edge. All this illustrates the point above that with "unknown unknowns" trial and error is a good way to proceed, but that takes time and extra money.

Governance

The word Governance is commonly used these days, and sometimes loosely. Just to be clear we need to understand that governance is not doing the work but ensuring the appropriate processes controls and measures are in place to provide the best outcome for the organization as a whole, and not the individual department or business unit. The following table may assist.

Governance	Management
Approve and prioritize investments	Set them up for delivery
Do right things (effectiveness)	Do things right (efficiency)
Monitor overall performance against business case	Provide information and review performance
Ensure appropriate practices in place to manage investments	Validate information and make decisions about investments delivery
Ensure appropriate structures and accountabilities are in place	Arrange structures and for processes to be developed
Ensure appropriate support is in place	Provide support to programs and projects
Ensure process are in place	Manage the process

A possible Framework for Governance which includes Risk Management at the overall corporate level and is shown in the diagram on page 52. It has five areas that Governance needs to consider in relation to new investments that the organization is planning to undertake. It is not just about having structures (committees, etc.) processes or roles and responsibilities, but also about ensuring accountability and leadership. Leadership is where management demonstrate by their actions their commitment to the organization's values. Accountability is about ensuring we are all held responsible for the stewardship of resources given to us. This not about blame but acceptance of responsibility for our actions, or lack of action.

Implementing Strategy		Demonstrating how proposed initiatives align with the organization strategy and will achieve the planned objectives	
Delivering Value	Structures, Roles & Responsibilities, Processes	Understanding linkages between initiatives & outcomes required to deliver benefits. Defining both achievement and benefit metrics for the whole life cycle	Leadership & Accountability
Managing Risk		Ensuring effective risk management processes are used in order to inform initial & on-going decisions on investments	
Measuring Performance		Providing appropriate processes to provide sound information to make effective decisions on delivery of initiatives	
Managing Resources		Assessing the organization's capability and capacity to plan and deliver the investment opportunity	

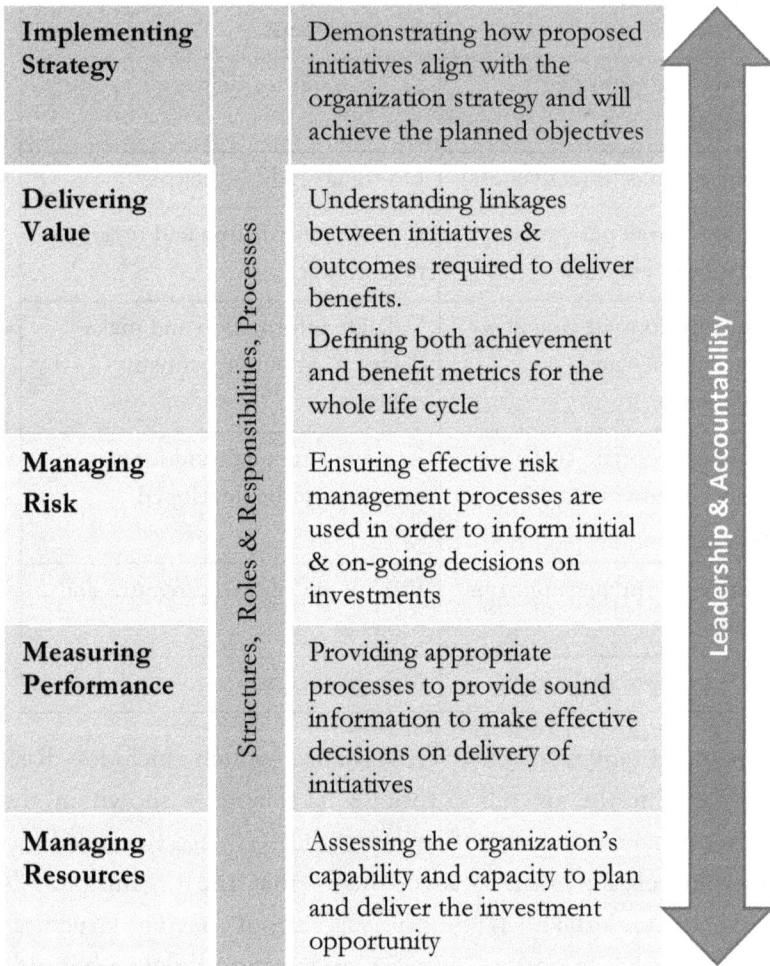

Figure 3 - Framework for Governance

I have quite a few Government Auditor General Reports in my collection, from countries around the world, all detailing significant project failures. It is interesting that all of them point to a failure of governance as a significant reason for the project failure and the loss of the public funds invested in it. In most cases the investment has been completely lost and nothing recouped. The Governance failure is typically because the Board or senior executive management did not exercise accountability and control and permitted conflicts of interest, poor performance by both their management and suppliers, and did not heed the early warnings provided to them by independent consultants or auditors. So having appropriate governance, which is not just about structures, processes or roles and responsibilities, but about leadership and accountability, which is critically important and the lack thereof is a major risk to the project investment. As mentioned elsewhere sometimes this also happens in the private sector and I have seen examples of it. However, there is nothing documented or available on it in the public domain that can be spoken about.

In 2010 I returned to Australia after living overseas for 4 years, and caught up on the local news to find that a major disaster was occurring in the Queensland state Health Department where a new payroll system had just been implemented. There were stories of staff being overpaid, underpaid, not paid at all and even ex-staff who had deceased being paid. It was a major debacle and an embarrassment to the Government but certainly helped to make the evening news more interesting as each day some new story of failure unfolded. The state Auditor General eventually issued a report, and a failure of governance was a significant reason. Ultimately there were also several government Commissions of Inquiry. What was meant to cost taxpayers $6 million is now estimated to have cost $1.2 billion dollars. The new payroll system which was meant to reduce the number of staff operating the payroll has actually increased it dramatically, and the system will need to be replaced. While a portion of the blame was laid at the feet of the external supplier, management of the government department and the state government IT services group came in for severe criticism for their failures and lack of accountability.

Reflections

This chapter has turned our attention toward some aspects of risk management that are usually given less focus. We need to be sure that we understand the problems that we are dealing with before trying to find an answer.

- Some types of risks such as "messy" and "wicked" ones will require us to adopt different approaches;
- Be wary of the optimism bias that we can all be subject to and ensure there are measures to counteract it;
- When projects are not going according to plan stop and do an objective evaluation and be careful of the "sunk cost syndrome" by spending more time and money to attempt to "retrieve" that already spent;
- Some risks may have a positive upside that can be exploited so look for them;
- If there are significant areas of uncertainty which may indicate unknown unknowns, there are alternative approaches to help uncover them and determine the appropriate response;
- Ensure that there is appropriate Governance in place over project initiatives to deliver the organizations benefits from the investment.

Endnotes

- Brooks, Frederick (1975) *"The Mythical Man Month - Essays in Software engineering"*, Addison-Wesley, Reading, Mass
- De Bono, Edward (1985, 1999) *Six Thinking Hats*, Little brown & Co, Boston
- Hancock, David (2010) *Tame, Messy and Wicked Risk Leadership*, Gower, Surrey

- Hancock, D & Holt, R (2003) "Tame messy and wicked problems in risk management", Manchester Metropolitan University Business School Working Paper Series (on-line), WPS054, Sept (accessed 11/1/15 http://citeseerx.ist.psu.edu/viewdoc/download?doi=10.1.1.110.9685 &rep=rep1&type=pdf)
- Keil, M & Montealegre, R (2000) "Cutting your losses: Extricating your organization when a big project goes awry", *Sloan Management Review*, Spring
- Loch, Christoph H, Solt, Michael E, & Bailey, Elaine M, (2008), "Diagnosing Unforeseeable Uncertainty in a New Venture", *The Journal of Product Innovation Management*, vol 25, pp 28-46
- Mintzberg, Henry (2004) *Managers not MBA's*, Berrett Koehler, San Francisco
- Perrow, C (1999) "Normal Accidents - living with High-Risk Technologies", 2nd Edn, Basic Books, NY,
- Project Management Institute, (2012) *A Guide to the Project Management Body of Knowledge (PMBoK Guide)*, 5th edn., PMI, Newtown Square, Penn.
- Queensland Health Payroll case – news articles on internet and YouTube, including the Auditor General's report.
- Rumsfeld, D (2002) see https://en.wikiquote.org/wiki/Donald_Rumsfeld
- Sharot, Tali (2011) *The Optimism Bias - A Tour of the Irrationally Positive Brain*, Pantheon Books, New York
- Snowden, David – see http://cognitive-edge.com/ for his numerous articles

CHAPTER 5

Improving Risk Management

"Human beings, who are almost unique in having the ability to learn from the experience of others, are also remarkable for their apparent disinclination to do so." (Douglas Adams - author of The Hitchhikers Guide to the Galaxy series)

Integration

On larger type projects where there are many people involved often certain aspects are handled by specific team members and it is difficult for one person to fully understand all the various components. For example one team member may be managing procurement, another focusing on risk, and other team members preparing quality plans, schedules and budgets. Each of them will have specialized skills in these areas. However, we want to make certain that decisions made in one area are captured in the plans for other areas. For example when working on risk management we will make certain decisions about what actions to take to reduce the likelihood or the impact of the risk, and this can be called containment or response actions. The effort for these actions and their cost needs to be included in both the schedule and the project budget. Decisions will be made about quality control actions to be taken when preparing the Quality Plan, and this work also needs to be included in both the schedule and the budget. They may also impact on risks.

The project is also not just about producing some outputs but how these will be integrated as part of operations and effort and budget will need to be allowed for this activity. This consideration of how one part of the project impacts on other parts is covered under the heading of Integration. Some of this is reasonably obvious and will be adequately covered, while other aspects of it may not be as obvious and maybe missed. The following table is an attempt to identify how problems in one area can impact on other aspects of the project.

Quality	Inadequate controls on quality of deliverables can lead to rework and potential schedule and cost overruns.
Procurement	Contracting out parts of the project normally means we have less control over delivery, however if the party is competent and reliable we can transfer some of our risk to them.
Schedule	The schedule will be a source of risk, however budget contingency derived from the risk plans needs to be factored back into the schedule, otherwise we will have the money but not the time to deal with the risks.
Cost	Cost estimates are a major source of risk, however having established sensible estimates it is still necessary to monitor against them regularly for potential overruns.
Scope	A common problem is starting design or build prior to having complete and agreed specifications, however overlapping is often performed to meet aggressive schedules. This can lead to rework later impacting on the schedule and budget.
Project Human Resources	While everybody agrees that obtaining the right resources on the project is vital, and will promise to provide them, they often do not appear on schedule, impacting on time, budget, quality and risk.

Communications	Getting decisions made by those who can realistically make them and ensure they are enforced, is a major challenge. Delays in decisions typically impact on both the schedule and budget and increase risk levels.
Integration	Integration complexity of the various components is often underrated and insufficient time allowed for it in the schedule.

Appropriate Approaches Based on Risk Profiles

Obviously we do not want a "one size fits all" type approach to risk management, so need to scale the time and effort spent on risk management to the risk profile of the project. Initially organizations used to do this by money value criteria. For example projects with the spend of less than 100k regarded as low risk, may be 100-1,500k as medium risk, and 1,500k and above as high risk. These values will need to be tailored to the size of the organizations and their capital spend. However, it soon became apparent that just money value was not a suitable criterion, since sometimes you could have a project with a small budget that had high potential risk. For example it could expose the organization to serious reputational risk if outcomes or schedules were not achieved as planned. Consequently today organizations will have a number of criteria that they used to determine the risk profile of the project, and therefore the appropriate level of management controls and overheads to be applied.

The criteria could include any of the following:

- Size of project budget;
- Project duration and especially if there is an immovable deadline or long duration both of which raise risk level;

- The number of the parties involved in the project at various stages, including external parties, with the larger number increasing the level of risk;
- Visibility of the outcomes in the public domain and the potential for reputation risk;
- The extent and level of change required in the organization in order to implement the project outputs, with more change considered as increasing the risk;
- Whether a new technology that has not been used before will be utilized on the project;
- Whether most of the project team will be co-located or if the project will be conducted across international boundaries which raises the level of risk;
- Any requirement for access to very specialized skills and their availability to meet the project timeframes.

Often there is a weighting applied to each of the criteria above, and then a rating for each of the items used, and an overall risk profile factor calculated. Depending on the number derived it will indicate whether the project is low, medium or high risk. For example a high risk profile would require more detailed and comprehensive risk management procedures, and also reporting to management on a more regular basis.

The Need for Collaboration

As some of our investments in projects become more dynamic, complicated or complex organisations struggle to successfully manage them to produce the desired outcomes. As a result, we are looking for improved ways to manage projects including changing our planning paradigms and alternative approaches to risk management. Numerous articles have been written on the topic including that mentioned in Chapter 4 on Heathrow Terminal 5 (Hancock & Holt, 2003) and another view by Thamhain (2013) commenting on the changing project environment says "an increasing number of organizations are complementing their analytical methods with managerial judgment and collective stakeholder experience, moving beyond a narrow dependence on just analytical models. ..... Examples are well known management tools,........... which rely mostly on organizational collaboration and collective judgment processes to manage the broad spectrum of risk variables that are dynamically distributed throughout the enterprise and its external environment".

Both authors note the need for greater collaboration to aid understanding and appropriate action.

Thamhain (2013) categorizes risks using different criteria but also recognizes the cascading effects of risk scenarios and how they can escalate through various categories to produce an enterprise impact.

Ultimately the point these authors make is that a traditional project risk register with plans for prevention and containment, and constant monitoring by the project team, is only part of the answer. The following diagram is my attempt to explain why we need a broad-based and collaborative approach to risk management across all levels of the organization.

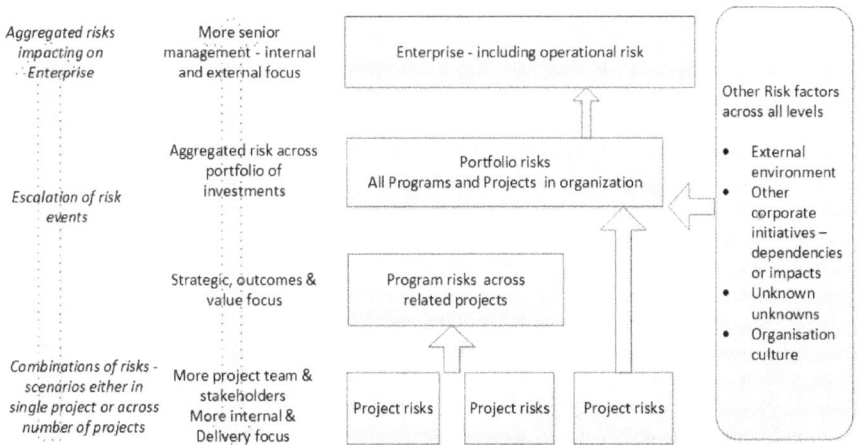

Figure 4 - Risk Levels and Scenarios

While the project team do need to be monitoring specific risks at that level and especially those concerned with delivery, there also needs to be an awareness and especially at higher levels, that these risks are not independent or confined to the individual project. When organizations combine related projects into a program to coordinate them better to achieve the desired outcomes, some of the risks are raised to the program level. At a portfolio level we see an aggregation of the risks of the various projects and programs which can produce a different picture of risk. Risk cannot be simply dealt with in organizational silos.

Collaboration at Work

Particular issues that need to be considered by all managers at various levels are:

- Low probability but high-impact risks need to be carefully monitored since if they do occur the impact is significant both on the project and more widespread. So it is important to ensure that the probability assessment is derived from a comprehensive range of inputs from many parties and regularly monitored for change. These risks can suffer from "weak signals" that are harder to detect than other more obvious risks.

- Linked risks in a project that are interdependent and can cause a chain of risks or risk scenario, with impact considerably greater than any of the individual risks within the linked scenario. (see Chapter 4 Risk Scenarios section);

- Also individual project risks can compound and escalate from an individual project to impact on the program, portfolio and even the enterprise. I can think of several major Australian banks who in the 80s and 90s undertaking large IT enabled projects (project cost range estimated at that time of more than $200 million) which spiraled out of control until shutdown and had a significant impact on the organizations for many years thereafter, and in one case had a detrimental effect on the bank's profitability. People closely associated with these significant initiatives found it severely damaged their reputations and careers.

- "Unknown unknown" risks are also potential but hard to identify, but some precautions can be taken such as multiple experiments to determine option feasibility and risk, but this requires time and resources which are often in short supply, at least until we have failed the first time around, and then are more willing to take suitable precautions on the second attempt. (See Chapter 4 Section on Unknown Unknowns);

- Lack of attention to the risk of achieving planned outcomes and benefits can lead to the project being a success on scope, time and cost criteria, but failing on the other more important score of delivery of business value.

The above situations therefore require a broad organizational perspective on risk going beyond any individual project or even program, and some larger organizations have introduced Chief Risk Officers, or an enterprise Risk Office to promote increased awareness and improved processes for managing risk, and also providing senior management with more visibility of significant risks. The focus here is on real collaboration between all parties.

There are many examples of how an individual project within an organization can escalate to cause enterprise level damage. Appropriate governance at the senior management level in the organization should be able to identify the risk that a project could fail and take suitable action both at the start and throughout its life, and before it becomes a disaster. Also the overall Board with external directors need to satisfy themselves that senior management have the appropriate checks and balances in place for risk management and they are being used.

The Victorian Ombudsman (Australian state of Victoria) produced a report in conjunction with the state Auditor-General (2011) on ICT –enabled projects and noted under the heading of Leadership, Accountability and Governance these key issues:

- Roles and responsibilities for ICT-enabled projects were often not clearly defined, acknowledged and accepted.
- Senior officers appeared reluctant to make critical decisions about projects.
- Many of the project steering committees did not have the requisite expertise.
- The Department of Treasury and Finance (DTF) could have taken a more pro-active role in many of the projects.

- The effectiveness of DTF's Gateway Review process was limited by its reliance on agencies engaging in and being supportive of the process, which often was not the case.

So the issues identified here by the Auditor-General are not about improving detailed project management process but Governance and parties working together to achieve the outcomes.

On the collaboration theme we need to move beyond the blame game, where project managers might claim events beyond their control, and senior management criticize project managers for poor planning and tracking, to an appreciation that no one party alone can fully understand either the causes or cumulative impacts of these interdependent risks emerging from dynamic, complicated or complex environments. As Hancock (2010) noted it will require a more behavioral and qualitative approach which will also include "challenging assumptions that risk is being managed separately by experts" and "encouraging conversations about risk" and "allow for contribution from across the organization by providing time and space for people to think and talk about risk". (Mookherjee & West, 2015)

This will be a challenge in organizations that want to still operate in a silo-based structure, since collaboration requires a willingness to explore alternative approaches with multiple parties and with reduced levels of control for some of the players, while still being accountable for outcomes. We need collaboration at all levels, team, project and other managers since no one person or group however smart can expect to understand the intricacies and causes and effects in these environments. Those in management roles often want to retain control, which is natural, but can inhibit effective collaboration. Instead we will need to rely heavily on the commitment of others, which for many is not necessarily a desirable place to be. As Martyn

Brown (2002) says in a complex environment managers need to "accept and be comfortable with the reality that we might be in charge but at the same time definitely not in control."

Collaboration can happen if senior management take action to create a culture of openness, trust, transparency and acceptance of accountability, and also demonstrate their commitment to these values by their on-going supportive actions.

Value of Lessons Learned

Some organizations are good at analyzing performance on their projects and capturing lessons learned for future use. However, other people argue that every project is different and that lessons are not necessarily transferable. I believe this depends on how you process the lessons and whether you abstract the principles that are important rather than the specific details. There are many excuses used for not learning from past lessons either in your own organization or in other organizations. You will hear comments like "we are different and this does not apply to us", "we understand what we are doing and know how to manage it", or "it will not happen to us as we know better" and so on. The reality is that they would benefit from observing these lessons as experience shows that the old saying "pride goes before a fall" holds very true.

As part of the approval of new initiatives the question can be asked of proposers by approving bodies "what lessons have been applied to this project based on learning from previous projects"? This can help to ensure that the question has been considered in preparing the plans.

Develop Organizational Processes and Conduct Training

Processes should help us to understand the steps to be taken and deliverables to be produced appropriate to the risk profile of the project, and indicate the tools and techniques to be considered. Staff need to be trained to use these processes and particularly to understand why they are using them, how they will be used, and the benefits arising from this. Management also need to be made aware of these processes not at the detail level but what they should be expecting and looking for from projects. If management do not show an awareness of and a commitment to the use of these processes, staff are unlikely to take them seriously. Over the years many project managers have said to me they spend considerable time in preparing project status reports but never receive any feedback from management, and therefore believe management do not read them. They therefore become very cynical about why they are producing the reports in the first place, and do not feel motivated to put considerable effort into reports that are not valued. Feedback can be in the form of questions about issues, which at least shows that you have read the report, and if there are no questions because the report is so comprehensive, then feedback to that effect is certainly worthwhile.

To be effective training needs to be based on practical application of the learning. Organizations today in order to reduce cost will often turn to on-line type training, which can suffer from lack of interaction with other people. However, on-line training can be supplemented with teamwork using a case study to develop practical applications. Even for management sitting in a workshop and listening is not sufficient engagement to ensure adequate understanding, and should be also supplemented with practical exercises. Understanding concepts is one thing but applying them to real life situations is another.

Software tools can assist but the complete Project Management toolsets often have limited capability without modification, and the specialized Risk tools may be more than you need. Start with a spreadsheet or even better a simple database until you finds the right level of risk management for your organization. Starting with complicated tools before you are ready can be frustrating so learn as you go and build understanding and confidence.

Measuring Performance

If our aim is to improve our performance in risk management over time then taking some measures of performance will certainly assist. Assessing risk management performance should be part of project closure activity and the subsequent report that is produced. Performance measures could include:

- The usage of schedule and budget contingency;
- Did additional risks occur that were not identified as part of the risk management process, and why?;
- How well the risk response actions were performed and how effective they were.

Some of these measures may be qualitative and some quantitative, but the important activity is to actually reflect on performance to discover what worked well and what did not work well, and how that might be changed in the future. Organizations that perform well in project management are constantly assessing their performance and improving based on the lessons they have learned. I am still amazed by the fact that many organizations continue to have repeat failures because they have not seriously reflected on their performance and tried to improve it. Improvement is more than just talking about it but taking the necessary actions to change processes and their controls.

However, as Henry Mintzberg (2011) tells us "don't be mesmerized by measurement", but use it to inform judgement.

"We Have No Choice But To Accept Risk"

I have come across many situations particularly among smaller organizations who feel that they have no choice but to accept the risks imposed on them by larger organizations since they desperately need the business to continue operating. This is particularly prevalent in Australia in the construction industry among contractors who take on risks beyond their ability to control and their capacity to absorb. It is even starting to happen amongst professional consultants also needing more work to continue in business. This is rather sad since it seems to me that it creates a downward spiral with very few winners in the longer term. Some clients are beginning to realize that by pushing too much risk on to their contractors/suppliers they are creating problems that may come back and hurt them later. However, not all clients have yet come to this realization.

It is not easy to provide easy answers to this situation. However, I will propose several potential solutions which might assist:

- Firstly ensure that your overheads are at an absolute minimum. They may have been built up over the years but can they be supported any longer?;
- Review whether you are delivering the very best of value to your clients, and this may require you to reconsider your business model and see whether there are additional activities that you can undertake for them at low cost but that deliver extra value to them;

- Develop an open relationship with your clients that allows them to see that you are delivering to them at the lowest possible cost while still allowing yourself a reasonable profit;
- Assure them of your transparency in all dealings which becomes especially critical during execution and key milestones;
- Discuss with them an appropriate and fair allocation of risk, and raise the problems of unfair risk distribution and its consequences;

Questions You Can Ask About Risk

There will be occasions when you as a manager will be approving new project initiatives and you will need to ask some probing questions about risk. Here are some suggestions.

- What was the process used to determine the estimates?
- Was any reference made to past experience to determine appropriate estimates?
- Were the estimators experienced in this type of project?
- Were the assumptions underlying the estimates examined to determine the level of risk?
- What parties were involved in the process of risk identification?
- Does the risk register contain risk from all potential sources, not just technical or delivery risks?
- What tools or techniques did you use in order to assess the probability or impact of significant risks in the risk register?
- If a quantified approach is used, explain the process to determine the recommended level of budget and schedule contingency?

- o Were schedule and budget Risk considered together?
- o Are Owners assigned to each risk? Do they understand their role?
- o How often will risks be reviewed?
- o Are there specific actions planned in order to control the risks?
- o Are the cost and effort for these planned control actions included in the budget and schedule?

All of these questions may prompt other questions, and the advantage is that all parties should have a more in-depth understanding of the risks, how they are derived and how they will be managed. Without this we are simply proceeding in a "blind faith" in achieving the desired outcomes.

Embed Risk in the Culture

Ultimately we want to risk management to be embedded in the culture of the organization. By that I mean that it becomes *"just the way we do things around here"* and not something special or an add-on or afterthought. However, for many organizations this means some change in the way things are done, and we know this is not easy since *"it deals with the complexity of human interactions"* (Harkrider and Tan, 2013). From their book the Change Facilitation Model shown in page 72 is taken. The book and the workshops KDi conduct can assist your organization to plan and adopt the necessary changes in order to implement improved Risk Management.

People are drivers of change in an organization

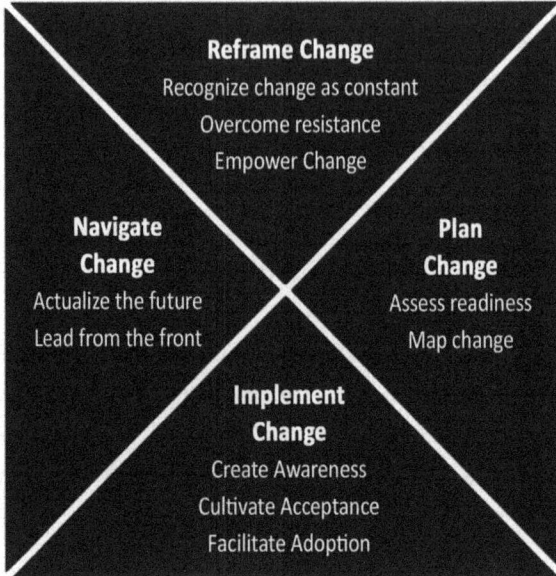

The leadership role changes in each phase of the model

Figure 5 - KDi's Change Facilitation Model

Reflections

- Risk management should not be a standalone exercise but its impact on all parts of the project planning and executing activities considered, including links with other organization processes such as those of finance, procurement, HR, audit etc.

- How do you ensure that Risk management is a collaborative exercise across all levels in the organization and recognize that as the risks aggregate upwards they became harder and more difficult to resolve individually and need collective attention and consideration by a number of parties.

- Rather than adopt a one size fits all approach, assess the risk profile of the project based on an agreed set of criteria, and then apply the appropriate level of rigor.
- Learn lessons from your own experience, and also those of others in your industry, and apply these to new initiatives to avoid repeating poor practices that can lead to failure;
- Develop effective processes and ensure that adequate training is provided, including at a management level so that all parties are committed to using them;
- Consider what risks the organization can effectively manage, and do not just accept risk because you do not believe you have any alternative. Consider carefully the options;
- To be effective risk management needs to be embedded in the culture of the organization so that it becomes the way work is performed, rather than an add-on or a "tick the box" exercise. To make this happen will normally require an organization change initiative to be planned and carefully executed.

Endnotes

- Brown, Martyn (2002) "Working with Complexity", The Ashridge Journal, Spring, The Ashridge Business School, UK
- Hancock, David (2010), Tame, Messy and Wicked Risk Leadership, Gower, Surrey UK
- Hancock, D & Holt, R (2003) "Tame messy and wicked problems in risk management", Manchester Metropolitan University Business School Working Paper Series (on-line), WPS054, Sept (accessed 11/1/15 http://citeseerx.ist.psu.edu/viewdoc/download?doi=10.1.1.110.9 685&rep=rep1&type=pdf)

- Harkrider, Nancy & Tan, Kim Leng (2013) *Leading Change that Matters – Making Adoption a Reality*, KDiAsia, Singapore
- Mintzberg, Henry (2011) *"Managing"*, Berrett-Koehler, SF
- Mookherjee, D & West, T (2015) "Working with Risk in Practice and Principle", The Ashridge Journal, Winter, Ashridge Business School, UK
- Thamhain, Hans (2013) "Managing Risk in Complex Projects:", Project Management Journal, Vol. 44, No. 2, April
- Victorian Ombudsman, (2011) Own motion investigation into ICT-enabled projects, In consultation with the Victorian Auditor-General, Victorian Government Printer, Nov - download from https://www.ombudsman.vic.gov.au/getattachment/d5e69dd1-400d-42cd-a570-9c6b21c4bb1e accessed 15/12/15

CHAPTER 6

Concluding Thoughts

"Mistakes are all right but failure is not. Failure is just mistakes you can't recover from; therefore, try and create contingency plans or alternate approaches for the items or plans that have high risk." (From: "100 Rules for NASA Project Managers" - collected and compiled by Jerry Madden, NASA Goddard Space Flight Centre, and edited by Rod Stewart, Mobile Data Services, Alabama, July 1996).

As mentioned in the Introduction I believe that today there is a lot more focus on risk management in organizations, and they are adopting more structured and quantitative approaches to understanding and managing the risk. There is certainly ample material resource available on the topic, some of which I have referred to in this thin book, which can help you improve the way that you manage risk. There is obviously some effort required to do this but generally when conducted at the appropriate level the payoff is worth the investment. That is not to say that in every case it is performed at an appropriate level since if not careful it can simply become a "tick-the-box" exercise and mostly a waste of time.

The benefits of good risk management are:

- reduces potential downside in projects;
- increases the potential upside in projects;
- allows for early and effective intervention when events do not go according to the plan;

- creates a positive culture of recognizing and managing risk, rather than punishing the innocent after the event;
- allows for new potentially risky initiatives to be undertaken with the requisite attention to the management of their risks.

However, as I also concluded in the Introduction we can be blinded by the science, as the bankers were in the GFC, so we need to heed the words of David Hancock (2010) *"... we need to move risk management from predominantly a science driven by numbers, systems and processes to an art with greater behavioral foundation"* especially when we face very complex situations with a number of parties involved each with their own agendas they are trying to achieve. Traditional risk management may be not completely suitable and you need to take more qualitative and collaborative approaches including partnering with others.

In the previous chapter I mentioned a number of approaches to improving risk management in your organization. Firstly you need to make an honest assessment of the level of your maturity. It is often assumed that management and staff fully understand the processes and techniques of risk management. I know that from my experience of teaching this subject at a university postgraduate level that many of my students believe they understand risk management until they undertake the course. At the end the students have a much deeper understanding of the subject matter, and we are mostly only dealing with the core fundamentals. I believe that many managers understand risk management at an intuitive level rather than understanding the fundamental processes and techniques. The knowledge of how the organization approaches risk and the expertise to manage it needs to be spread throughout the organization if it is to be fully effective. Organizations sometimes set up risk management offices, but use these groups to build up internal capability rather than have everybody rely on a centralized risk office.

Some larger organizations engage risk consultants which is good if you are undertaking significant projects (say hundreds of millions or billions of dollars) otherwise you will need to build your own internal capability.

Hopefully by reading this book it has given you an overview of the management of risk and encouraged you to "dig deeper" on some specific areas which are of interest to you.

Endnotes

* Hancock, David (2010) *Tame, Messy and Wicked Risk Leadership*, Gower, Surrey

RESOURCES

<u>References to standards</u>

- ISO 31000:2009 Risk Management standard – available from
  http://www.iso.org/iso/home/standards/iso31000.htm
- A Guide to the Project Management Body of Knowledge (PMBoK) – Chapter on Risk management - available from the Project Management Institute. (www.pmi.org)
- Practice Standard for Risk Management - available from the Project Management Institute. (www.pmi.org)
- Project Risk Analysis and Management Guide (PRAM) – available from APM (UK Professional Project Management body) https://www.apm.org.uk/PRAMGuide

<u>These web sites will provide further information on cases of project failures:</u>

Calleam Consulting http://calleam.com/WTPF/

Omega Centre - Transport cases:
http://www.omegacentre.bartlett.ucl.ac.uk/publications/omega-case-studies/

"They Meant Well – Government Project Disasters"
by D. R. Myddelton, published by The Institute of Economic Affairs – download from:
http://www.iea.org.uk/publications/research/they-meant-well-government-project-disasters

Web sites – these sites contain useful article that you can download free of charge

- Risk Doctor - http://www.risk-doctor.com/
- Max Wideman - http://www.maxwideman.com/
- AACEi (Association for the Advancement of Cost Engineering International) - professional body for project controls engineers. They have a number of good practices on risk management suitable for the practitioner but you will need to register to be able to download these. (http://www.aacei.org/)

Risk Management steps and outputs produced (Refer to Chapter 3). This is more detailed table of the summary in that chapter.

Activity	Possible Inputs	Possible approaches	Output	Who is involved
Plan Risk Management (defining how to conduct risk management activities for the specific project)	Feasibility Study / Business Case (internal) or a Contract (external). Standard Templates.	Analytical techniques. Meetings.	Risk Management Plan. Decision on Risk Register Template to be used.	PM
Identify Risks (determine which risks affect the project & document their characteristics)	Risk Plan, other project documents, reviews of documented assumptions. Risk Management Plan. WBS or Work Breakdown Structure.	Document Reviews. Checklists. Brain-storming. Facilitated Workshops. Historical data.	Unqualified list of all identified risks placed into Risk Register.	PM & Team Sponsor Stakeholders

Activity	Possible Inputs	Possible approaches	Output	Who is involved
Perform Qualitative Risk Analysis (prioritize risks for further analysis or action by assessing and combining their probability of occurrence and impact)		Rating Assessment criteria. Checklists. Risk Matrix. (often Probability and Impact assessed as Low, Medium or High and then prioritize)	Updated Risk Register with qualified list of risks with probability & impact documented. Impact areas also documented e.g. cost, schedule, performance etc. Some risks identified for further treatment.	PM & Team
Perform Quantitative Risk Analysis (numerical analyze of the effect of identified risks on overall project objectives)	Risk Plan & Register. Project Time/ Resource Plan.	What if planning including: Critical Path Method Delphi Technique Historical Data EMV, Decision trees	Quantified List of Risk in Risk Register – i.e. Factored Risks using expected monetary value (EMV).	PM & Team

Activity	Possible Inputs	Possible approaches	Output	Who is involved
Plan Risk Responses (develop options and actions to enhance opportunities and to reduce threats to project objectives)	Risk Register with factored Risks. Risk Thresholds.	Normal Risk strategies. Checklist. Brainstorming. Historical Data. Peer review.	Updated Risk Plan / Risk Register with mitigations/ actions etc. Budgets for mitigation and contingency – in Project Plan. Estimated residual risk after treatment. Contingency plans if risk occurs.	PM & Team Independent Reviewer
Control Risks (implement risk response plans, track identified risks, monitor residual risks, identify new risks and evaluate risk process effectiveness throughout the project)	Risk Plan & Register. Status Reports. Project Audits. Contract change notices. Other triggers.	Frequent Review of Risk Register. Review effectiveness of mitigations.	Updated Risk Register with: • New Risk • New Mitigations/ Actions • Closed Risks (Return through the above process for new risks). Status Reports with Risk status.	PM Team Sponsor Stakeholders

Activity	Possible Inputs	Possible approaches	Output	Who is involved
Baseline Risk Plan and Register (these are established during project planning but once approved become the baseline and become living documents that require frequent review throughout the life of the project)	Risk Plan. Risk Register. Project Start-up. Checklists. Review Checklists.		Project Approval – Key Risk sheet. Approved Project Plan with Risk Register. Approved Risk Plan.	PM Sponsor Stakeholders

Author

Harold Ainsworth has held senior management positions in several project service organizations involving oversight of large complex projects, and been responsible for several organization change management initiatives. Also he has considerable experience as a consultant and educator in portfolio, program and project management in both Australia and South East Asia. His current consulting work is in helping organizations achieve sustainable value from their strategic investments through effective Governance, and the practices of portfolio, program and project management.

Harold holds post-graduate qualifications in management and is a member of four professional organizations, and he teaches part-time at two Australian Universities in their graduate Project Management Programs.

www.ingramcontent.com/pod-product-compliance
Lightning Source LLC
Chambersburg PA
CBHW071115210326
41519CB00020B/6300